No Pun Intended

Volume Too

.

By

WILL LIVINGSTON

This book is a work of fiction. Any resemblance to actual events, locales, or persons, living or dead, is entirely coincidental.

Published by Original Life Saver Publishing

paperback ISBN: 978-1-957141-13-8

Printed in the United States of America

Cover design by Jonathan Brendan

Editor and Illustrator: Elsie Bloomfield

Typesetting: Book Design Inc.

DOWNLOAD FREE NOW

GET this Image
and More Tricks
For the Last of Us
⟶

Scan This Code
or Visit >>

https://bit.ly/ellieorjoel

It doesn't matter how much you push the envelope.

It'll still be stationary.

What did the Confederate soldiers use to eat off of?

Civil ware.

What did they use to drink with?

Cups... Dixie Cups.

I walked into my sister's room and tripped on a bra.

It was a booby-trap.

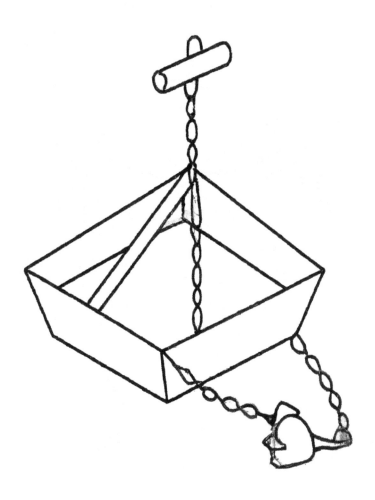

A book just fell on my head,

I only have my shelf to blame.

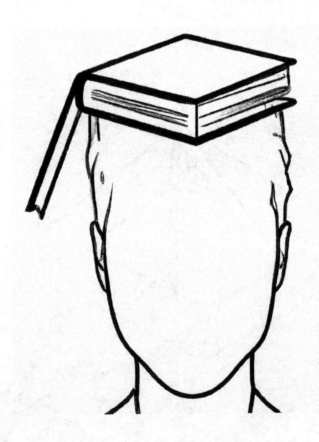

What is the leading cause of divorce in long-term marriages?

A stalemate.

Bakers trade bread recipes on a
knead-to-know basis.

A moon rock tastes better than an earthly rock
 because it's a meteor.

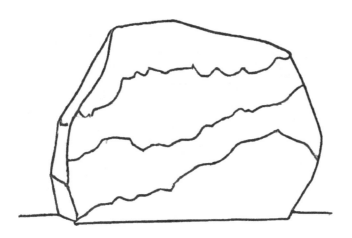

A backwards poet writes inverse.

AVFESISIVE

I used to be addicted to soap.

But I'm clean now.

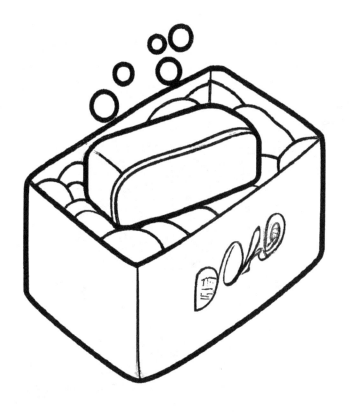

3.14% of sailors are Pi Rates.

I stayed up all night wondering where the sun went.

Then it dawned on me.

What did the mermaid wear to her math class?

An algae bra.

Why did the scarecrow get a promotion?

He was outstanding in his field.

Tried to catch some fog earlier.

I mist.

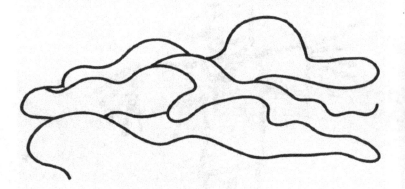

What does a pirate say while eating sushi?

Ahoy! Pass me some soy!

You wanna hear a joke about pizza?

Never mind, it was too cheesy.

If a dish towel could tell a joke,...

I think it would have a dry sense of humor

What did the green grape say to the purple grape?

Breathe, you idiot!

Why can't a nose be 12 inches?

Because then it would be a foot.

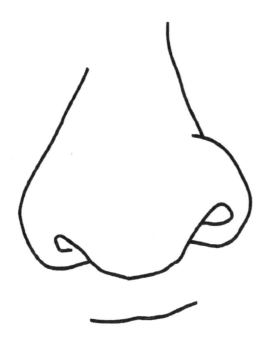

A boiled egg in the morning is

really hard to beat.

I'm reading a book about anti-gravity.

It's impossible to put down.

I'm glad I know sign language.

It's become quite handy.

I forgot how to throw a boomerang.

But it came back to me.

When the clock is hungry...

It goes back four seconds.

I once heard a joke about amnesia...

But I forget how it goes.

When the power went out at the school...

The children... were de-lighted.

Those fish were shy.

They were obviously coy.

The frustrated cannibal

threw up his hands.

I didn't have the faintest idea...

as to why I passed out.

There was once a crossed-eyed teacher...

who had issues controlling his pupils.

Diarrhea is hereditary...

It runs in your jeans.

I heard two peanuts walk into a park...

One was as-salted.

What is a pirate's favorite letter?

'Tis the C."

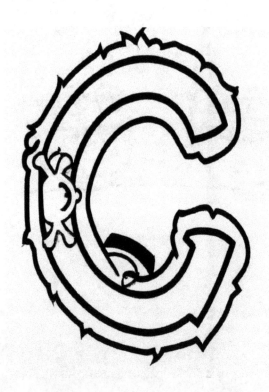

Those two men drinking battery acid

will soon be charged.

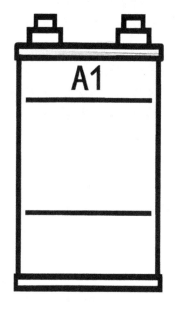

The midget psychic escaped prison.

He was a small medium at large.

I'm inclined...

to be laid back.

Newspaper headline reads: "Cartoonist found dead at home..." details are sketchy.

The Magician got frustrated and

pulled his hare out.

A criminal`s best asset... is his lie-ability.

I heard about the guy who got hit in the head with a can of soda.

He is lucky it was a soft drink.

It's not that the guy didn't know how to *juggle*...

He just didn't have the *balls* to do it.

You know what's not right?

Left.

What did the triangle say to the circle?

You're so pointless.

What did the cannibal get when he showed up to the party late?

A cold shoulder!

Why did the tomato turn red?

Because it saw the salad dressing!

I told my wife she was drawing her eyebrows too high.

She looked surprised.

I can't believe I got fired from the calendar factory.

All I did was take a day off.

Why don't scientists trust atoms?

Because they make up everything.

What do you call fake spaghetti?

An impasta.

I used to play piano by ear, but now I use my hands.

Why do seagulls fly over the sea?

Because if they flew over the bay, they'd be bagels!

What did the grape say when it got stepped on?

Nothing, it just let out a little wine.

I'm reading a book on the history of glue.

I just can't seem to put it down.

Why did the scarecrow win an award?

Because he was outstanding in his field.

I'm on a whiskey diet.

I've lost three days already.

Did you hear about the Italian chef who died?

He pasta way.

I'm reading a book on gravity.

It's so hard to put down.

I don't trust people who do acupuncture.

They're back stabbers.

Did you hear about the guy who lost his left arm and leg in a car crash?

He's all right now.

I can't believe I got fired from the bank. They told me I wasn't a good fit.

But I'm convinced it's because I kept asking customers if they wanted to see my savings.

I used to be a baker,

but I couldn't make enough dough.

Why did the banana go to the doctor?

Because it wasn't peeling well.

I'm reading a book
on anti-gravity.

It's impossible to put down.

I don't trust people
who take drugs.

They're always up to
something.

Why did the chicken cross the playground?

To get to the other slide.

I'm reading a book about teleportation.

It's bound to take me places.

Why did the hipster burn his tongue?

He drank his coffee before it was cool.

I used to be a shoe salesman,

but I got the boot.

What did the grape say when it got stepped on multiple times?

Nothing, it just let out a little whine.

Why did the man run around his bed?

To catch up on his sleep.

Why did the bicycle fall over?

Because it was two-tired.

Why don't skeletons fight each other?

They don't have the guts.

I used to have a fear of hurdles,

but I got over it.

What do you get when you cross a snowman and a shark?

Frostbite.

I'm really good at sleeping.

I can do it with my eyes closed.

Why do chicken coops only have two doors?

Because if they had four, they would be a chicken sedan.

Did you hear about the kidnapping at the playground?

They woke up.

I'm reading a book on the history of glue.

I just can't seem to put it down.

What did the janitor say when he jumped out of the closet?

"Supplies!"

Why did the math book look so sad?

Because it had too many problems.

Why do they call it a "building" when it's already been built?

Shouldn't it be called a "built"?

I'm writing a book on how to reverse identity theft.

It's a steal.

Why don't oysters share their pearls?

Because they're shellfish.

What did the grape say when it got stepped on?

Nothing, it just let out a little wine.

I'm on a whiskey diet.

I've lost three days already.

Did you hear about the man who was cooled to absolute zero?

He's OK now.

I tried to organize a professional hide and seek tournament, but it was a complete failure. Good players are hard to find.

I went to a seafood disco last week

and pulled a mussel.

Why do birds fly south for the winter?

Because it's too far to walk.

I used to play piano by ear, but now I use my hands.

I'm reading a book on the history of clocks.

It's about time.

Why do cows have hooves instead of feet?

Because they lactose.

I'm writing a book on the perils of drinking.

It's a shot in the dark.

What did one wall say to the other?

"I'll meet you at the corner."

I'm reading a book on teleportation.

It's bound to take me places.

I'm on a new diet.

I only eat cookies that are still in the oven.

Why did the man put his money in the freezer?

He wanted cold hard cash.

I'm reading a book about submarines.

It's underwhelming.

I went to a party dressed as a piñata.

I was beaten up.

Why did the grape stop in the middle of the road?

Because it ran out of juice.

Why did the chicken cross the playground?

To get to the other slide.

I'm reading a book on the history of glue.

I just can't seem to put it down.

Why don't vampires drink beer?

Because it's too bloody.

What did the fish say when it swam into a wall?

"Dam."

I'm writing a book on the art of comedy.

It's a laugh a minute.

Why did the coffee file a police report?

It got mugged.

Why did the scarecrow win an award?

Because he was outstanding in his field.

I used to be a shoe salesman,

but I got the boot.

I'm writing a book on the benefits of exercise.

It's a real page-turner.

Why did the gym close down?

It just didn't work out.

I'm reading a book on how to solve crimes.

It's a real whodunit.

Why don't skeletons fight each other?

They don't have the guts.

CPSIA information can be obtained
at www.ICGtesting.com
Printed in the USA
LVHW052233200623
750269LV00028B/229